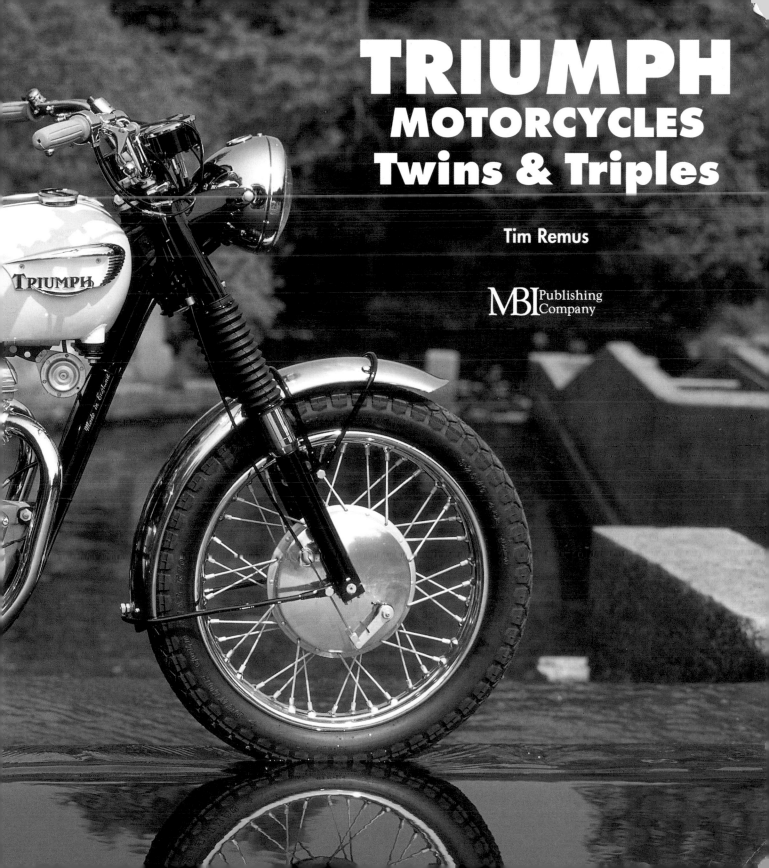

# TRIUMPH
## MOTORCYCLES
## Twins & Triples

Tim Remus

MBI Publishing
Company

First published in 1997 by MBI Publishing Company, 729 Prospect Avenue, PO Box 1, Osceola, WI 54020-0001 USA

© Timothy Remus, 1997

All rights reserved. With the exception of quoting brief passages for the purposes of review, no part of this publication may be reproduced without prior written permission from the Publisher.

The information in this book is true and complete to the best of our knowledge. All recommendations are made without any guarantee on the part of the author or Publisher, who also disclaim any liability incurred in connection with the use of this data or specific details.

We recognize that some words, model names and designations, for example, mentioned herein are the property of the trademark holder. We use them for identification purposes only. This is not an official publication.

MBI Publishing Company books are also available at discounts in bulk quantity for industrial or sales-promotional use. For details write to Special Sales Manager at Motorbooks International Wholesalers & Distributors, 729 Prospect Avenue, PO Box 1, Osceola, WI 54020-0001 USA.

Library of Congress Cataloging-in-Publication Data
Remus, Timothy
  Triumph motorcycles : twins and triples /
  Timothy Remus.
    p.   cm. — (Enthusiast color series)
  Includes index.
  ISBN 0-7603-0312-6 (alk. paper)
  1. Triumph motorcycle—History. I. Title.  II. Series.
TL448.T7R44  1997                          97-8684
629.227'5'09—dc21

**On the front cover**: Most Triumph enthusiasts consider the 650-cc twins built from 1968–1970 to be the epitome of the breed. A strong double-leading shoe front brake complemented the engine's higher output. This fine TR6 belongs to Bobby Sullivan.
**On the frontispiece**: Classic Triumph brochure cover art from 1950.
**On the title page**: Reflected beauty. Mid-1960s Bonneville possessed a flow of line surpassed by few other motorcycle makers. Another winner from the Bobby Sullivan collection.
**On the back cover**: The last year for the production triple (barring the new Triumphs) was 1976. The T160 Trident was a smooth, reliable road-burner, displacing 750 cc. Owner John McCron restored this handsome Trident over a five-year period.

Printed in China

# CONTENTS

# ACKNOWLEDGMENTS

This collection of Triumphs, both old and new, has come together, "with a little help from my friends." That list of friends is long and should start with Bobby Sullivan, the man who reintroduced me to Triumph motorcycles. Garry Chitwood, the man who restores most of Bobby's bikes, helped too, by answering my questions and proofreading the manuscript.

The other bike owner of note is Dick Brown. Dick made his bikes available, rolled them here, there and everywhere, and even convinced the guys at the local elevator to let us photograph his Blackbird on their loading platform. Collectively, I must thank all the other bike owners, like Al Charles, Dave Flory, Jaye Strait, Mike Benolken, Rodney Birosh, Jim Godo, Ron Peter, Randy Baxter, and Mike Lunsford.

A number of the bikes seen here were photographed at the Mid-Ohio race track during AMA's Vintage Days. The stewards and security people at Mid-Ohio couldn't have been any more helpful and always found a way to accommodate my requests to photograph on or near the track.

The number 59 race bike is owned by The Motorcycle Heritage Museum, located at AMA headquarters in Westerville, Ohio. Jim Rogers, director of the museum, helped me roll the rare race bike into position and then provided the technical material I needed for the captions.

John and Tom Healy not only made their bike available for photographs in Daytona, but also helped me move and position Dick Brown's two T100 bikes during the Vintage Days event.

Some authors guard their special knowledge the way the CIA takes care of state secrets. Then there are those like Lindsay Brooke, who always acted flattered that I should call and happy to share with me his wealth of Triumph knowledge.

Not all the bikes were photographed on the East Coast or in Ohio. Local Minneapolis/St. Paul restorer Steve Hamel helped me find bikes like the very nice T160 restored by John McCron and the T150 owned by Delano Sport Center just west of Minneapolis

The new Triumphs are represented here as well. I'm grateful to Michael Lock, former CEO of Triumph Motorcycles America Limited, for allowing me to take four of the new Triumphs out for photography—and sorry I was so late in bringing back the 1200 Daytona.

I close with a thanks to my lovely and talented wife, Mary Lanz. Mary proofreads manuscripts and runs to the photo lab when I don't have time. More important than that, she helps to lift my spirits when I get bogged down in a book that I don't think will ever get finished.

*Tim Remus*

# INTRODUCTION

Like every kid who grew up in America in the 1960s, I soon learned that there were only two really cool bikes to own, the Triumph Bonneville and the Harley-Davidson Sportster. But I couldn't buy a Bonneville, or even a beat-up old Tiger, because Mom and Dad laid it right on the line: "no motorcycles."

During high school I worked at a car wash, and one of the older guys named Louie had a Bonneville. On slow days Louie let me ride the bike up and down the driveway. That doesn't sound like much now, but for a sophomore in high school it was better than a date with a cheerleader.

That might have been the end of my lusting (for Triumphs anyway) if it hadn't been for Bobby Sullivan. When I met Bobby he was looking for someone to photograph his collection of Triumphs. Bobby's passion for Triumphs somehow rekindled my own, earlier fascination. During all the hours we photographed his collection for the Sullivan Brothers Calendar, I became well acquainted with Triumphs. Out of the work I did for Bobby Sullivan came the desire to do this book.

The book itself is an overview of Triumph motorcycles, from the first Speed Twin of 1938 to the amazing T595 Daytona. The bikes themselves are a mix, some are the most famous while others could be called the most obscure. Though I don't guarantee the accuracy of the bikes, most have been lovingly restored by people who take their work and their hobby very seriously. Whenever possible the captions note the occasional use of non-original parts.

For me, the best part of assembling this book has been meeting the people who own and restore the bikes, and sharing in their excitement. Next best was being able to photograph the bikes—to try and capture on film the beauty and visual harmony that typifies most Triumph designs. From the carefully designed engine covers to the lovely, tapered gas tanks, the parts on a Triumph all seem to fit the bike and complement each other. If the bikes were ugly, I wouldn't have so many extra transparencies tucked away in the notebooks.

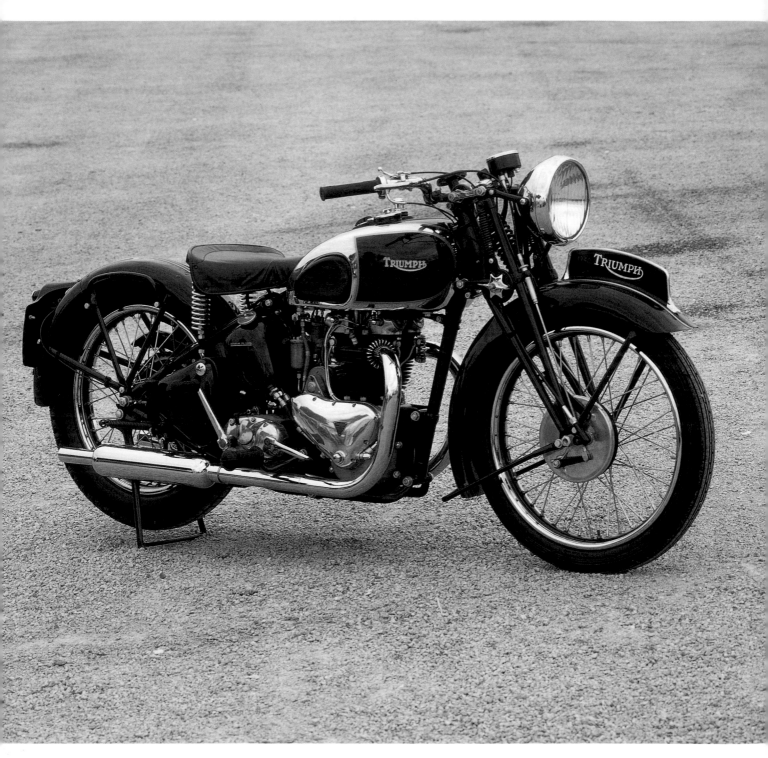

# CHAPTER 1

# SPEED TWINS AND EARLY BIKES

## *The First Real Triumph*

Though historians might insist that we begin the story of Triumph motorcycles in 1902, when the first single-cylinder motorcycle was manufactured, the history as understood by the vehicle's enthusiasts really started not with a date but a model.

The model is the Speed Twin, designed by the legendary Edward Turner. Displacing 500 cc, this new vertical twin weighed no more than the single-cylinder bikes of the day, yet offered significantly more horsepower and torque. In the best hot-rod tradition the new vertical twin engine was stuffed into a frame designed for a Triumph single. To help the new bike stand out from those mundane thumpers, the first Speed Twins were offered in only one color—Amaranth Red with chrome trim.

Here in 1938 was a 365-pound motorcycle with 26 horsepower that would easily rev beyond 5,000 rpm. All this at a time when the motorcycle market was dominated by heavy two- and four-cylinder models, or lightweight singles. No bigger than one of those singles and faster than many of the larger V-twins, the Triumph Speed Twin quickly became the giant-killer of its day. Edward Turner worked at Ariel before coming to Triumph, and before that he ran a motorcycle shop of his own. Like another visionary designer best known for his Model T automobile, Turner understood that good designs should be simple, light, and durable.

Turner's new Speed Twin used a three-piece, 360-degree crankshaft set into vertically split cast-aluminum crankcases. At either end of the crankshaft a large ball bearing provided support, with the central weight bolted in between the two crank "halves." Instead of using roller bearings on the big ends of the connecting rods, Turner specified the rods be made from an alloy that could run right on the crankshaft without the need for bearing inserts. He used two camshafts, one in front and one behind the one-piece cylinder barrel. The cams were identical and interchangeable.

The cast-iron cylinder barrel was topped by a one-piece cylinder-head assembly. Six studs held the barrel to the crankcases while eight studs united it with the head. By casting the cylinders and head each in one piece, Edward Turner designed an engine that was both strong and light.

The bore and stroke measured 63 x 80 mm, for an undersquare design. The two intake ports ran parallel to each other and were fed by a single Amal Type 6 carburetor with a 15/16-inch bore.

The 1940 Speed Twin was essentially the same as the first 1938 model, right down to the Amaranth Red paint. The girder fork shows its check springs, which were new that year.

Stylish in its day, Triumph's prewar gas tank had its ammeter and oil pressure gauge located in the tank top, along with the light switch and a removable inspection light. The speedometer resides in its own housing above the headlight.

A single-row primary chain took the Twin's power to a four-speed transmission. Both the transmission and clutch assembly were borrowed from the largest of the Triumph singles.

The hardtail frame was borrowed from the same line. Its single front downtube split into twin tubes that formed a cradle under the new engine and ran back below the transmission, while a single top tube passed from the steering neck to the seat. A girder fork provided the front suspension while a sprung seat took the place of rear suspension—still many years away at that point.

With valenced fenders, a large-diameter headlight, and a gas tank with the gauges mounted on the top plate, the Speed Twin proved to be both fast and stylish.

All new designs have their "teething problems," yet the new Turner-designed twin had relatively few. The primary change made for the second year of production was increasing the number of studs used to locate the cylinders to the crankcases. Thus the 1939 and later Speed Twins are often referred to as "eight-stud" machines while the earliest models are known as "six-stud" Twins.

There was, of course, more power to be had from the early Speed Twin design, and in 1939 Triumph announced a new model, the Tiger 100. By raising the compression from 7.2:1 to 8:1 and porting the cylinder head, engineers could get the new twin to easily top 100 miles per hour.

To separate the new model from the similar-looking Speed Twin, the sporty Tiger 100 wore a silver paint job with black pinstriping.

Further development of the new vertical twins would have to wait until after the war. In fact, the war did more than interrupt the development of civilian products. All work at the Coventry factory came to a stop in November 14, 1940, when the plant was leveled during an early German air raid. Thus the early war years were spent in temporary facilities located at Warwick and later in the new plant in Meriden located outside Coventry.

Despite the difficulties of setting up production in a temporary facility, Triumph did produce a large number of military bikes during the war. The air raid destroyed all the tooling for a new military bike known as the 3TW. This was to be a 350-cc overhead-valve twin with a unitized three-speed gearbox.

Bikes produced during the war for the military included the 3HW, a 350-cc thumper with overhead valves, and later the TRW, a flathead 500-cc twin. Based on the earlier 3H, the 3HW came to the military complete with rigid frame and olive-drab paint.

Rear wheel measures 19 inches while the front is 20 inches in diameter. Triangular-shaped tool box mounts to the frame while the oil tank sits under the seat across from the battery. Early Triumphs did not use a folding kick-start pedal.

To economize on production, the new flat-head TRW shared internal dimensions and many components with the overhead-valve 500-cc twins. Instead of using two camshafts, the TRW used one, which ran across the front of the crankcases. With low-compression, 5:1 pistons, the flathead was well suited to slow-speed use and would run on almost any grade of gasoline.

11

With the exception of the flathead engine, the TRW is similar to other Triumphs of the time. The engine used a typical gear set to drive the camshafts, located in the normal position. Tool box and oil tank are all standard issue Triumph items, the gas tank even carries the signature parcel grid.

ingenuity of certain motorcycle enthusiasts within the Triumph factory.

One such enthusiast, Freddie Clarke, then an amateur racer and head of Triumph's Experimental Department, combined the lightweight "generator" top end with a standard Tiger 100 bottom end. The net effect was a lightweight Tiger 100 and a first place in the 1946 Senior Manx Grand Prix. The success of Freddie's hybrid racer eventually forced the factory to offer the Grand Prix model.

Two years later the factory used the same basic recipe when it built three special bikes for use in the International Six Day Trials. Though the bikes were hastily assembled, their riders came away from the ISDT with three individual gold

medals and the Manufacturer's Team Trophy. The factory specials used full-size Speed Twin frames, but the new TR5 "Trophy" model offered in late 1948 came with its own shorter-wheelbase frame.

This TRW dates from 1954, though the TRW military motorcycle was designed and first built during World War II. The engine is a 500-cc vertical twin, similar to many Triumph engines except that this design is a flathead. Of note is the early use of the telescopic front fork. Originally these bikes came with a simple pillion pad for the passenger—an earlier owner of this bike installed the sprung saddle for the benefit of his sweetheart's derriere.

Famed racer Dick Mann has campaigned this 1948 Trophy TR5. This example used the shorter wheelbase frame, and the special 500-cc engine created by mating a standard bottom end to the "generator" top end. Among the many upgrades on this example are rubber fork gaiters, which replace the original steel shrouds.

Perhaps the best of the new postwar Triumphs, at least from an American perspective, was a bike known as the Thunderbird. If Edward Turner had achieved his first major success by dropping a hot twin into the space normally occupied by a slower single, he accomplished his next major splash by increasing the displacement of the already-fast 500-cc twin to a full 650 cc.

Thus with the war over and the decade nearing the end, Triumph was well positioned to answer the needs of civilian motorcyclists looking for more power and faster speeds.

# CHAPTER 2

# EVOLUTION OF A GREAT DESIGN

## The Fast, Furious Fifties

The American perspective on power and speed might best be summed up by that old adage: "A little too much is almost enough." With that basic attitude the American market was not easily satisfied with faster and faster 500-cc Triumph twins. Edward Turner was a man keenly aware of the importance of the American market, and early in 1949 he ordered the works department to begin creation of a bigger Triumph twin.

What the R&D department at the Meriden plant put together might be called a "bore and stroke" job in American street slang. Starting with a standard Speed Twin engine, the boys at the factory first built a special crankshaft with an additional 2 mm of stroke. Next, the standard cylinders were bored from the stock 63 mm to 71 mm. The true beauty of the plan lay in the ease with which it was implemented. The new crank still fit in standard crankcases and the stock cast-iron cylinder barrel contained enough extra "meat" that the new bore size could be accommodated without changing the casting.

This "black bird" is one of a limited number of Thunderbirds that were painted black at the factory at the request of American dealers. Whether in black or blue, this 650cc Triumph was both stylish and fast.

The four-bar badge was first used in 1950. In this case the gold and chrome works very well against the black background.

### The New Thunderbird

Thus the new 650 engine (the dimensions actually worked out to 649 cc) could be easily dropped into any existing Speed Twin or Tiger 100 frame. Even in a mild state of tune, the single-carburetor 650 made well over 30 horsepower. The Thunderbird name was a stroke of Edward Turner's genius, borrowed in this case from a motel he saw in South Carolina during one of his many trips to the States. Introduced in 1950, the Thunderbird was the high-speed cruiser of the day—essentially

By the time this 1953 T-bird was built, other makes offered true rear suspension. Triumph relied on the sprung hub like this one, mounted in a hardtail frame, until introducing its own swingarm frame in 1954.

a Speed Twin with more displacement, a larger Amal carburetor, and a blue paint job. This was a bike that would easily run near the century mark without complaint.

If the engine would not complain, however, the rider might, for the first Thunderbirds came with telescopic front suspension and a hardtail frame. In answer to riders' requests for rear suspension Triumph offered a "sprung hub." This consisted of a large rear-wheel hub assembly that allowed nearly two inches of vertical travel as the machine passed

over bumps. Though the other English brands offered bikes with true rear suspension during this same period, Triumph didn't offer a swingarm rear suspension until 1954, on the Tiger 100 and 110.

The increase in horsepower created the need for a better gearbox. Thus the new Thunderbird featured a revised four-speed transmission with stronger gears and a clutch assembly with one additional plate. The new transmission also offered a drive for the speedometer, which was no longer driven by the rear wheel since the advent of the sprung hub.

Still in a hardtail frame, this 1952 TR5 uses the Triumph sprung hub in the rear. Headlight is designed to be easily removed so the bike can be used in off-road events.

The new model came with the headlight nacelle, actually introduced one year earlier on the road bikes. With the speedometer and gauges moved to the headlight housing, the top of the tank was no longer needed for gauges. In place of the tank-mounted gauges came the optional tank-top parcel grid, which was destined to become another Triumph trademark.

## A Hotter Hot Rod

By the time the swingarm frames were available, the "Blue Bird" was no longer the hot rod of the Triumph line. Following the earlier pattern, a hopped-up Thunderbird was made available in 1954 and named the Tiger 110. By adding high-compression pistons, ported heads, more radical camshafts and a larger carburetor, the 650's output was raised to 42 horsepower.

This TR5 Trophy carries the later close-pitch-fin cylinders and head in place of the square-barrel "generator" parts used on earlier examples. The 500-cc engine relied on one Amal 6 carburetor with remote float bowl and a Siamesed exhaust system.

The early Trophys were almost too pretty to take off-road—the desert-dueling days are over for this carefully restored 1952 example.

Not just any old side hack, the Swallow features torsion-bar suspension and a true knock-off hub. Note the neat clearance light on the fender.

The new road rocket also offered a more modern appearance with the combined tool box, air cleaner, oil tank, and battery case. Otherwise the Tiger 110 carried the same tank insignia with the four horizontal stripes running across the front of the tank, and a headlight and gauges contained in one trademark headlight nacelle.

If the Thunderbird could easily hit 100, the new Tiger 110 was capable of running over 110 miles per hour. With the new swingarm frame, the Tiger 110 was quite the machine in its day.

Early in the new decade changes were announced for the 500-cc twins as well. Primary among these was the new head and barrel, both die cast in aluminum alloy. These new alloy castings had more fins per inch than earlier castings and came to be known as "fine pitch" or "close pitch." This head and cylinder set also replaced the "generator" top ends used on many early Trophy models. The bottom end of these smaller twins was to remain essentially unchanged until the new unit-construction engines were introduced in 1957.

For Tiger 100 owners who wanted still more power there was always the racing kit available from the factory. Comprehensive in the extreme, this kit included two carburetors, high-compression pistons, high-lift camshafts, new valve springs, a

More than just a hopped up T-bird, the 650-cc T110 used a more robust crankshaft supported by ball bearings on either end and heavy-duty connecting rods. Extra power came from higher compression, different intake cam and larger carb than those used on the Thunderbird. Ventilated 8-inch front brake is the same one used on the smaller T100.

A lovely combination including a 1954 Tiger T110 with then-new rear suspension and a Swallow "Jet 80" side car. Though the German Steib side cars were more common in the United States, this English-made Swallow certainly looks at home alongside the hot rod of the 1954 Triumph line.

This unrestored 1956 T110 is near perfect. At a recent show the bike only lost points for having the wrong mufflers. The 1956 model carries the twinseat first introduced in 1954 and the same 8-inch brake seen on the earlier model.

tachometer, new exhaust pipes with megaphones, and all necessary cables and brackets.

For 1953, a new model was offered, the T100C. Essentially a T100 with the racing kit installed at the factory, this new bike came with all the parts normally found in the racing kit: the twin carbs, racing camshafts, and a larger-capacity oil tank.

In 1956, Triumph made a number of significant improvements to the twins. The company made available for the 650-cc engines a new cylinder head, known as the Delta head. This new aluminum head saved weight, eliminated the external oil drain pipes and allowed the engine to run a slightly higher compression ratio.

More exciting than a new cylinder head was the introduction of a new model. The TR6 Trophy combined the new 650 engine and Delta head in a go-anywhere bike equipped with a small, detachable headlight and small gas tank.

In fact, 1956 was a banner year for Triumph all around. Not only was the company selling 500- and 650-cc twins in record numbers, but the bikes also earned the World Motorcycle Speed Record after Johnny Allen hit 214 miles per hour at the Bonneville Salt Flats.

But what Americans really wanted in the late 1950s was a twin-carb 650-cc Triumph. Although two-carburetor heads were available for the 500-cc twins for some years, it wasn't until 1958 that a true twin-carb head became available in the Triumph catalog for the 650-cc twins. More carbs meant more power at higher revs, resulting in more load on all the internal engine components. To handle the additional loads in more and more powerful engines, the 650-cc twins gained a new one-piece forged crankshaft one year later.

## The Most American of English Motorcycles

Evolution works for machines as well as animals. With the Triumph's new twin carb head and a recent record at the Salt Flats, a new model seemed to be in order. For 1959 Triumph announced the bike that would always mean "Triumph" to a generation of Americans. the Bonneville or T120. Essentially this was a T110 fitted with the new head. With two carburetors and a boost in compression, the new Bonneville put out a full 46 horses. The first year Bonneville was the only one to come with the headlight nacelle housing the speedometer and gauges.

Americans did indeed love the speed of the new Bonneville, though the styling left many wishing Triumph had put the two carburetors on the TR6 instead of the new model. In fact, many Triumph buyers did exactly that—they bought a new TR6 and then added the factory's twin-carb head with an extra carburetor. A legend isn't born overnight, and the 1959 introduction of the Bonneville might be called a still-birth. In 1960 the

The 1956 T110 received Triumph's new aluminum alloy Delta cylinder head. Its design eliminated the external oil drains used on earlier heads. The carburetor is an Amal Monobloc, introduced on Triumph twins in 1955.

# Dick Brown

If you ask Dick Brown how he first became involved with motorcycles, he states simply, "Motorcycles have always been part of my life. Hell, my grandmother rode a motorcycle in the days when that was really rare. My father had motorcycles; we had three-wheel Servi-cars at the shop that the mechanics rode out to service calls."

Though his first bike was a 125-cc Harley-Davidson, Dick moved to Triumphs when he started enduro riding. "My first Triumph was a Cub," he says; "I started enduro riding with that in the mid-1960s as a 'B' rider. After only about three races I became an 'A' rider and the next year I moved up to a 500-cc Triumph." Dick became good enough to win three state championships on Triumph trials bikes before a broken leg and the call to adult responsibilities at the family John Deere dealership brought his enduro riding to an end.

Like most enduro riders, Dick did all his own wrenching on his bikes, and that experience served him well some years later when he began collecting old Triumphs.

"I bought a beat-up 500-cc bike at a farm sale one day," recalls Dick. "I paid seventy-five dollars for it and I just couldn't wait to get it home and hear it run. Well, of course it burned oil, so I rebuilt the engine and then I got the rest of the bike fixed up and looking real nice. For a while it became a crusade—I thought I was put on this earth to find all the old Triumphs and bring them back to life. Eventually I realized there just isn't time to fix all those bikes, so now I concentrate on the ones I really like."

Today Dick owns about 35 Triumphs, but some of those aren't too complete. If you ask him which he favors, he answers that the TR5 is the one he likes best. But after a pause he adds that the Blackbird (Thunderbird) is pretty neat, too. Then, of course, there's the T110 with the sidecar . . .

Mention of the T110 brings up a story about the way the combination came together. After

Dick Brown's 500-cc TRW is one of his favorite bikes for running errands near home or at one of the many Triumph meets he attends each year.

restoring the T110 Tiger, Dick took it to shows and often brought back a trophy for Best in Class, but never Best of Show. A friend suggested he build something "unusual" as a way of getting the attention of the judges. This same friend knew the location of a certain Swallow sidecar in the hayloft of an old barn. Dick knew a good idea when he heard it. Since restoring the sidecar and matching it to the T110, Dick has taken home at least 10 Best of Show trophies.

You might think a successful guy like Dick Brown would be farming out the work by now and simply managing the collection. Wrong. Dick does nearly all the work of rebuilding and restoring the bikes in his collection himself. If you call him at home in the evening, you're probably interrupting the work that goes on in his small home shop. When there's something he can't do alone, or simply isn't good at, he calls on his good friend Bill Danison. Bill helps with things like fabricating parts that can't be purchased and painting the bikes in the correct factory colors.

Dick's current "hot button" is a Grand Prix he's putting together. "The engine is an original Grand Prix unit," he says. "But it was shipped to the States as a spare; it was never mounted in a frame. I've got a frame that's pretty much the correct one, but when I put the two together I won't present it as an original Grand Prix; I don't think that's right."

For Dick the real fun of any restoration project is the work itself. "I work hard to get the bike done, to assemble it with all the right parts," he says. "But once a particular bike is finished, it's not nearly as important to me as when I'm working on it."

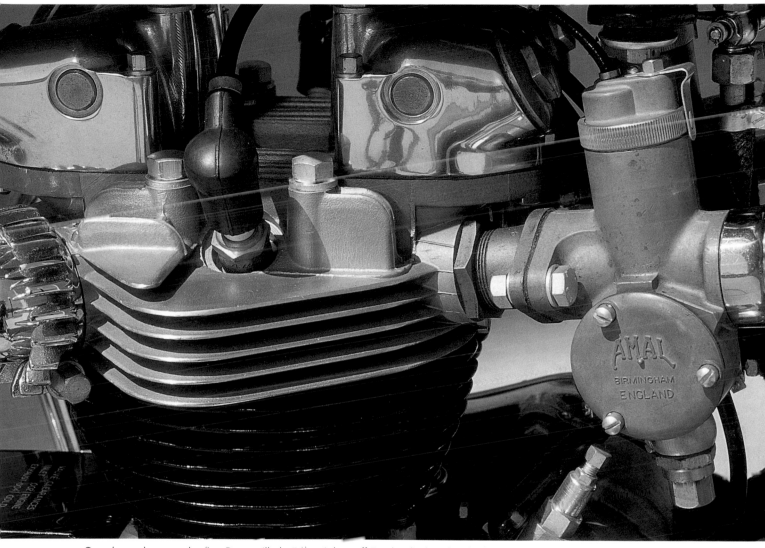

Overdressed or not, the first Bonneville had the right stuff "under the hood." The big news was the twin-carb head equipped with Amal Monobloc carburetors fed from a single, remote float bowl.

Bonneville came back, with the same two carburetors and new TR6-style sheet metal.

In 1957, Triumph introduced a new unit-construction 350-cc twin known as the 3TA. The new engine was soon enlarged to 500 cc and later given a new twin-carb cylinder head known as the "Delta" head. The Delta head, with its splayed ports, set the pattern for the larger twins as well and helped fuel demand for a twin-carb head for the 650-cc models. In 1958 Triumph offered a special 500-cc twin known as the TR5AD, the first unit 500-cc twin to come with the twin carb head as standard equipment. Though Americans on the street always seemed to prefer the larger 650-cc

Most Americans think of Triumph Bonnevilles as lean hot rods with slim fenders and a chrome headlight housing. But this fine example from 1959 shows us the truth—the first Bonneville came to the beach party in a tuxedo when everyone expected a T-shirt and jeans. Note the single-downtube frame, which changed to the duplex design in 1960.

twins, the new 500-cc unit engine would go on to make quite a name for Triumph on American flat-track and road-race courses.

As the 1950s drew to a close, Triumph could point to many successes: the new 500-cc engine, a twin-carb 650-cc model, record sales, and a reputation for high quality. But as good as things were, the best was yet to come.

The first-year Bonneville retained the signature headlight nacelle, with integral gauges combined with valenced fenders on both ends.

Though originally introduced in 1957 as a single-carb 350, the new "unit" engine was soon enlarged to 500 cc and treated to standard hop-up techniques. After winning the most prestigious American race with their new 500 in 1962 and 1966, Triumph named its fastest 500-cc model Daytona for 1967.

# CHAPTER 3

# BABY BOOMER BIKES

## *Wild on the Streets*

The Wild and Crazy decade of the 1960s started well for Triumph. Not only did it have the new Bonneville 650-cc twin, but a new unit-construction 500-cc twin as well. Some would say these were, "the best of years" for Triumph Motorcycles, but there would also be a few rough spots along this otherwise smooth and successful highway.

### Extra Sheet Metal for the New 500

In the fall of 1957, the new model Twenty-One twins arrived at most Triumph showrooms. Displacing 350 cc, this new model offered a variety of new features, not all of which were welcome on the American side of the Atlantic. Yes, the unitized engine and gearbox would prove both durable and fast. The styling, however, was another matter. By having an enclosed rear wheel in a sheet metal creation known as a "bathtub," the bikes took on a dumpy and very un-Triumph-like appearance. The enclosed rear wheel and skirted front fenders were intended to offer increased weather protection for serious riders. Americans, however, thought the extra sheet metal a servicing hindrance and an ugly addition to an otherwise attractive motorcycle.

The 1968 Bonneville used the new BSA Group twin-leading shoe front brake and taillight housing. The Amal Concentric carburetors were introduced on the Bonnie in mid-1967.

Even the larger Tiger 650-cc models were fitted with this "foul" weather gear that Americans found so unattractive. The new Edward Turner designs proved so unpopular that many new bikes were converted back to "standard" form by the dealers before they were rolled out onto the show floor.

If the sheet metal was ruled a failure, the unit-construction 350-cc engine was to prove a winner in a literal sense. In many ways the new, smaller twin followed standard Triumph practice with a three-piece forged crank, connecting rods with two-piece big-ends, two camshafts in the standard positions, cast-iron, one-piece cylinders, and a one-piece cylinder head cast in aluminum.

The new 350 was designated the 3TA, and was soon followed by a 500-cc version known as

### Following

Looking like a miniature Bonneville, the 1967 T100R was listed in U.S. Triumph literature as the Daytona Super Sports, though it still wore Tiger 100 toolbox badges. It features twin carbs with chrome aircleaners. Tires are from Avon, 3.25 x 19 front and 4.00 x 18 rear. The finned ignition points cover is nonstandard. This Tiger uses glue-on rather than bolt-on knee pads. The hot T100 came with both a tachometer and speedometer.

The same only different—two 500-cc twins, a 1968 Daytona in the foreground and a single-carb T100 behind. In 1968 the first "Daytona" designation on toolbox transfers appeared.

the 5TA. Triumph enlarged the 350 by increasing the bore size from 58.25 to 69 mm, while retaining the same 65.5-mm stroke. This produced a robust, oversquare 500-cc twin.

The increase in displacement provided more power, which was still housed in all that extra sheet metal. Edward Turner did respond, if slowly, and in 1961 Triumph offered the TR5AR and TR5AC (R for roadster, C for competition). With single carb cylinder heads and no sign of a bathtub or skirted fender, these bikes paved the way for a variety of Triumph 500-cc models to follow.

The 500-cc twins were steadily improved throughout the model's life. Once the sheet-metal wheel enclosures were removed, the bikes regained their good looks. By 1963 the 500-cc twins relied on coil ignition for spark, with the points located under a small cover on the timing gear side and driven by the exhaust camshaft.

If the 500-cc twins were less popular than the 650s on American streets, they were certainly successful on the race track. During most of the 1960s AMA Grand National racing was still run under the old Class C rule. These rules decreed that, for road racing and flat tracks, flathead engines (read: Harley-Davidson) could displace up to 750 cc, while overhead valve engines, with their superior breathing, could displace only 500 cc.

Despite the disadvantage of reduced cubic inches, the new 5TA-based twin proved to be a formidable weapon on U.S. racetracks. To keep Triumph name plates in the winner's circle, the distributors from both coasts offered specially modified 500-cc racing engines. The enthusiasm of the factory, distributors and dealers for racing paid big dividends for Triumph. In 1961, a Triumph 500 ridden by Don Burnett placed second in the Daytona 200. The following year, Burnett won the race. In 1964, Gary Nixon won the Sacramento Mile flat track race and placed second at Daytona.

The success of the 500-cc twins spawned a new model, the Daytona. Technically known as the T100R, and designated the Daytona in 1968, the new 500 came with a special twin-carb head designed with different valve angles for better breathing and more-efficient combustion. In addition to the Daytona, the 500-cc bikes came in model designations similar to those used on the big twins. A small C model, for example, featured a single carburetor and raised exhaust pipes that ran along the bike's left side.

In 1967, the small-twin line received a new, more robust frame, and the following year the twin-carb bikes received an eight-inch, single leading-shoe front brake.

The late 1950s were the height of Triumph's sheet-metal mania. Even the new T120 Bonneville was introduced in 1959 with deeply valenced fenders and the traditional Triumph headlight nacelle. And though the bikes were fast, many buyers opted to sidestep the Bonneville's styling by buying a TR6 and adapting the twin-carb cylinder head.

Though they might not have been lightning quick to react to the American preference for a very "basic" bike, Edward Turner and the management at Triumph did eventually follow the advice offered by their distributors and dealers.

The 1960 Bonneville, actually designated the TR7/A and TR7/B (high- and low-pipe models) for the United States, came with a bare headlight housing and simple, non-valenced fenders. Leftover 1959 models were still designated as 1960 T120 Bonnevilles in the new catalog. Unfortunately the 1960 through 1962 Bonnevilles used the "Duplex" frame with twin front down tubes. The first of these new frames cracked near the neck, until a reinforcing tube was added that ran from the top of the two down tubes to the single top tube. Eventually the Duplex frame was replaced entirely with a new single down tube frame in 1963.

## Unit-Construction 650

The new single down-tube frame of 1963 supported an even larger development, the unit-construction 650-cc engine. The new "big" Triumph twin followed the design lead of the smaller, 500-cc twins introduced six years earlier. The new crankcases offered more support in a lighter package. Changes included a new cylinder head, one more fin on the cylinder casting, ball-bearing main

In 1963 the 650-cc twins changed from the duplex frame to the single-downtube design. This 1963 bike uses coil ignition, with the points housed under the round cover on the engine's right side and driven by the exhaust camshaft. Restored by Garry Chitwood at C&S Cycles in Bassett, Virginia, and painted by Dave Perewitz, this TR6 probably looks better now than it did in 1963.

alternator stator and the use of a cross-over tube between the two exhaust pipes.

By the end of the 1960s, the Bonneville and TR6 were about as good as they were likely to get. Based on a design more than 30 years old, the Triumph vertical twin had achieved the zenith of its development. Purists feel the 1970 models—the last ones manufactured before the advent of the oil-in-frame models—were the last and best TR6 and Bonnevilles that Triumph made.

The next decade would see an abundance of changes, but not necessarily improvements, in the Triumph twin.

The Bonneville evolved slowly during the mid-1960s, as evidenced by this example from 1965. This 1965 Bonneville is the last year T120 equipped with the chrome parcel grid mounted to the tank—as much a part of Triumphs as the vertical twin engine.

Though still a Bonneville, the 1967 model had evolved considerably from the models of the early 1960s. Note the Aubergine (a metallic maroon) and white paint, the taillight and the "eyebrow" tank badge.

The 1965 Bonneville used a Smiths magnetic speedometer and tachometer, rotating in different directions.

# A Passion for Triumphs: Bobby Sullivan

If you ask Bobby Sullivan how he came to collect so many Triumphs, he recalls an incident in 1988 that started the whole thing. "There was this 1973 Triumph in the paper for three hundred dollars; I bought it just on a whim and that's when it all began. At that point I hadn't ridden a bike for 15 years. The bike ran, so I took it for a ride and it was a real kick. It took me back 20 years, put a flame back in my life."

What Bobby calls his next "mistake" was attending a Jerry Wood auction in Daytona. When he came home from Daytona that year, there were two more Triumphs in the trailer, a restored 1963 Bonneville and another Bonneville, this one an unrestored 1970 model. During the time Bobby was in Daytona, he met a young restorer named Garry Chitwood from Bassett, Virginia. Though he didn't know it at the time, Bobby was destined to do a significant amount of business with Mr. Chitwood.

Today Bobby Sullivan owns more than 20 very desirable Triumphs. His personal collection includes two 1948 Speed Twins, nearly every Bonneville produced from 1959 to 1970, and a series of TR6s. In order to keep all those bikes running and provide material for future restorations, there are another 40 or so bikes in pieces and a rather significant parts inventory.

To understand how it happened and why it happened so quickly, you have to understand Bobby Sullivan, his background, his Irish enthusiasm, and his tendency to do things "all the way."

Bobby's passion for Triumphs actually started in 1969, the year he was slated to graduate from tech school with a degree as an aircraft mechanic. Aircraft mechanics were pulling down $6 per hour at the time, which didn't seem too bad until Bobby discovered that a good motorcycle mechanic could make three times that much working flat rate. Before long he was the Triumph mechanic at a Honda and Triumph dealership in Nyack, New York.

As Bobby explains it, "The shop had some old parts bikes in the basement and when things were slow I put a couple of those together and raced them in the scrambles. In the winter when things were slow, my brother and I would go to the West Coast, racing and wrenching as we went."

It was a few years later that Bobby discovered there was more than one way to win at racing. By this time the two-stroke bikes were giving the Triumphs a hard run for their money. Bobby started bringing a case of two-stroke oil to the races and selling it to his competitors. One case led to two or three and soon Bobby added knobby tires to the inventory in the back of his van.

Distribution was the next logical step and with help from his wife, Arla, he mailed out flyers and the kitchen table became the shipping department. Never one to pass up an opportunity, Bobby added helmets to his line of goods, gave up racing, and never looked back. Today, Sullivan Brothers is one of the biggest importers of helmets in the country.

Which brings us back to the present, a time when the success of Sullivan Brothers leaves Bobby looking for an excuse to break away from the business and sneak into the basement and limber up all those special Triumph tools in his old toolbox. "The first few bikes I restored turned out kind of rough," he admits. "I've gotten more patient, though, and right now I'm working on a 1948 Speed Twin that Arla found as a basket case. I've also come to do a lot of work with Garry Chitwood. Garry does great work: he has good attention to detail and he always gets the right parts on the right bike."

Getting the right chain guard on a 1968 Bonneville, for example, isn't as easy as it sounds. "The English did things in a funny way," says Bobby. "They might order 2,000 chain guards of a certain style, but no one knew exactly when they ran out of that style and changed to a slightly different guard. We might

A look down into the den at Bobby and Arla Sullivan's house.

know the change happened during 1968, but it could have started with bike number 300 or bike number 600. For some of the parts, no one really knows. Even the judges at the shows don't know."

Bobby has his own troubles with the judges when he takes two or three bikes to a show, but not for having the wrong chain guard. The points Bobby loses are for having bikes that are "over-restored." The paint in particular, often applied by Dave Perewitz from Cycle Fab in Brockton, Massachusetts, is flawless. As one judge put it recently, "those bikes were never that pretty when they came from the factory."

For Bobby Sullivan, it isn't winning that makes this obsession worthwhile, it's something else. "What I enjoy the most is when I buy one that's been sitting in a damp garage for fifteen years and it's got a rod hanging out the bottom of the case. I mean a really junky, rusty old bike. And then six months or a

year later it looks brand-new, I've brought it back to life. That feels really good."

Asked if he has a favorite, Bobby confesses to a certain weakness for the 1968, 1969, and 1970 models. His goal for the collection? "Well, I'm missing a few that I'd really like to have, like a 1964 T120C, one of the rarest of Bonnevilles."

Bobby's Triumph collection is sometimes pressed into duty as part of the business, either as part of the Sullivan Brothers calendar or in one of the catalogs. Despite their promotional use and the increasing value of the collection, Bobby swears this isn't about money.

"The prices of the bikes keep going up and it's gotten to be a pretty big investment, but they're not for sale," he says. "Not the bikes and not the parts. I do it just to see the bikes come back to life. That's what's in it for me."

# CHAPTER 4

# TRIPLES AND THE LAST OF THE TWINS

## *The Last of the Best*

Despite the upheaval, the revolving-door management teams, and the frequent work stoppages that plagued Triumph during the 1970s, the company continued to produce functional motorcycles well into the 1980s. Both the 500- and 650-cc twins continued through this period, along with their new three-cylinder stablemate known as the Trident and later 750-cc twins.

### The Daytona Winner Rolls on and on

Through the turmoil of the late 1960s, the small 500-cc twins were left pretty much alone. Even when the larger twins were restyled to no good effect, their smaller brethren were left with their timeless good looks and balanced performance intact.

The 500-cc twins changed little during the late 1960s and early 1970s. The premier version remained the twin-carb T100R Daytona. For competition work, the C model was still in the line with upswept pipes running along the bike's left side.

One of the few additions to the small-twin line during this period was the new TR5T Trophy Trail. The new off-road Triumph was created for 1973 by combining a BSA frame with the single-carb 500-cc Triumph engine, a wide-ratio four-speed gearbox and an aluminum gas tank. With a 19-inch tire in front and an 18-inch in the rear, both equipped with knobby tires, the new TR5T was more dirt bike than earlier Trophy or C models.

Unfortunately, about the time this model was beginning to come off the line, the workers shut down the Meriden plant and so it never produced the bike in large numbers. By the time the plant was up and running again, it only produced the big twins.

### Bigger, Faster 650 Twins

1971 was the year Triumph's owners, the BSA Group, introduced the "restyled" Bonneville and TR6. It was a case of fixing something that wasn't broken. The new frames raised the seat height three inches and in place of the old full-width front drum brake, the new Bonnevilles offered a new "conical" drum brake and slimline fork. The new bikes came with a long list of "improvements," including a flat-back headlight housing with wire supports and new side covers.

Even with the extra cylinder, a Trident is still a slim, well-proportioned machine.

**Following**
The T160 was the last of the three-cylinder line. Though still a 750-cc engine, the last triples used the canted-cylinder, BSA-style powerplant.

One of Triumph's "last gasps," the TSS eight-valve engine was offered in 1982, just before the final closing of the Meriden factory. The new head, mated to new aluminum-alloy cylinders with higher-compression flat-top pistons netted 60 horsepower—a long way from the 26 horses of the first Speed Twin! *Lindsay Brooke*

More useful than the unwanted sheet metal was the new five-speed transmission first offered as an option in 1971. One year later it was standard equipment. By 1972 most of the visual changes instituted in 1971 were undone. The big twins now came with smaller gas tanks, a modified version of the new frame with a lower seat height, and a traditional headlight housing.

The big news for 1973 was the long-awaited 750-cc twins. For years the aftermarket had been offering big-bore kits designed to create a 750 twin. In fact, Triumph offered 200 special, T120RT 750-cc twins in 1970, but these were built from aftermarket parts and intended only to homologate a 750 twin for AMA's new 750-cc rule (which replaced the old 750/500 Class C rule).

Under the primary cover is the T160's duplex chain (the T150 used a triplex) and a modified clutch assembly with an outer gear that engages the electric starter. Like the earlier T150, the last triples used three Amal Concentric carburetors.

This 1974 TR5T Trophy Trail, a bike that was taken out of the crate and never ridden. The engine used in the Trophy Trail is the well-known 500-cc vertical twin, used here in a mild state of tune with only one Amal carburetor. The four-speed gearbox, with lower ratios than the street Daytona, and knobby tires measuring 21 inches in front and 18 in the rear mean this Trophy is well suited to work in the dirt. Tape seen on fender is part of the protective packaging used on the bike during shipping.

The 750-cc Bonneville, now known as a T140V, retained its twin carbs while the Tiger (TR7RV) got only one. The enlarged twins came with new cylinders, a new cylinder head, lower compression, and new camshafts. Because of the bike's extra power, the duplex primary chain used previously was replaced by a triplex chain and all the new bikes came with the five-speed transmission. Even better, the "new" drum brake was finally replaced by a proper Lockheed disc brake.

The first of the new 750s actually used a bore and stroke of 75 x 82 mm for a total displacement of only 724 cc. Later in the 1973 model year, different cylinder castings had to be specified before the bore could be opened up to 76 mm, for a total displacement of 744 cc.

The bikes produced at the Meriden plant (now a co-operative owned by the Triumph workers) from 1975 to the end of production in 1983 were mostly variations on the 750 Bonneville

theme. In 1976, a rear disc brake was added, and in 1977 the Silver Jubilee edition, commemorating the twenty-fifth year of Queen Elizabeth II's reign, was assembled and sold as a limited edition.

The next year's American model, the T140E, came with new Mark 2 Amal Concentric carburetors and a new cylinder head so the bike could meet new, more restrictive U.S. emissions laws. Eventually the Bonneville gained cast wheels, electronic ignition, and even an electric starter late in its life.

Between 1980 and the Meriden plant's closing in 1983, Triumph continued to produce the familiar 750-cc twin and a number of new variants intended to increase sales. One was a 750 Tiger Trail; another, the less-expensive 650-cc Thunderbird. Near the end, the co-op produced a special eight-valve twin known as the TSS and even a prototype twin with overhead cams and liquid cooling.

But it was all for naught. In 1983, with debts piling up, the Meriden factory, built during World War II, closed for good. However, that's not the end of the Triumph story—and not even the end of the Bonneville story.

Englishman John Bloor bought the Triumph name and rights and then licensed aftermarket parts maker Les Harris to produce Bonnevilles— the machine that even after 14 years of production just wouldn't die.

The 1977 Silver Jubilee was built in limited numbers (only 1,000 for the U.S. market) to commemorate the twenty-fifth year of Queen Elizabeth II's reign. Technically, this Bonneville is a T140V, meaning a 750-cc model with the five-speed transmission. This Bonneville uses the later oil-bearing frame and the forks without gaiters.

**Following**
This 1973 Hurricane retains all its Craig-Vetter inspired style. The "real" gas tank is hidden under the flowing gas tank/side cover combination, which is molded fiberglass. Originally designed as a BSA, the Hurricane uses the BSA version of the BSA/Triumph three-cylinder engine, with the cylinders canted forward.

To differentiate the Jubilee from other Triumphs, each one used chrome-plated timing and primary cases, chromed rims with painted centers, its own unique paint job, Dunlop red-line tires, and a certificate of ownership.

The T150 used the Triumph version of the three-cylinder engine, one with vertical cylinders. Oil cooler, unique to the triples, kept the bigger engine cool under pressure. Aftermarket mufflers are from Dunstall, and very similar to those that came on the bike when new.

This T150 triple was built in 1973 thus it carries all the right styling cues—a proper Triumph gas tank, convex side covers, and 3-into-2 exhaust.

# CHAPTER 5

# RACING TWINS AND TRIPLES

## *Winners on Nearly Any Surface*

Triumph motorcycles have been raced since the first bikes were built. As soon as there were Speed Twins there were owners willing and eager to try them out against the guy with the Harley—or the flathead Ford roadster. Because World War II put a crimp on most racing activities, the real story of Triumph's triumphs on the racetracks starts after 1945.

### Generator Triumphs:
### The Grand Prix and Trophy

One of the first noteworthy Triumph racers was built in the factory development shop shortly after the war by Freddie Clarke. Freddie's partner in this clandestine endeavor was Ernie Lyons, fellow employee and amateur racer who came up with the idea of building a modified Tiger 100 for road racing.

Their efforts were done "on the sly" because Mr. Triumph, Edward Turner, was opposed to building race specials or supporting racing at the factory level. Despite his opposition, Triumph motorcycles were raced in nearly every type of racing on both sides of the Atlantic Ocean, often with some degree of factory support.

For 1967 the factory T100Rs gained a better fairing with better aerodynamics than the year before and a fiberglass 5.25-gallon gas tank instead of the alloy BSA item used in 1966.

Clarke started with the fastest Triumph in the lineup, the Tiger 100. To save weight, the aluminum top end from the wartime generator engine was used. Though the poor gasoline of the day wouldn't allow for a high compression ratio, Clarke did port the heads and install twin Amal carburetors fed from a single float chamber. Racing camshafts and solid pushrods helped to round out the breathing improvements. Spark was by racing magneto and the tachometer was driven by an adapter off the exhaust camshaft.

The standard four-speed transmission was used with a set of close-ratio gears and driven by the standard primary chain. The frame for the new racer was essentially stock, with a few modifications to mount the rear-set pegs. For suspension Clarke added one of Triumph's new sprung hubs at the rear and a set of telescopic forks in front. With abbreviated fenders and a plate to show the bike's number, the new race bike was ready to run.

And run it did. All the way to first place in the 1946 Manx Grand Prix. More success followed until finally, in 1949, Turner agreed to produce a race-replica bike for sale to the general public. Much like the first prototype, the new factory Grand Prix used the Tiger frame, sprung hub and modified Tiger engine with a "generator" top end. The bottom end of the new engine was left mostly stock, though heavy-duty versions of the alloy con-

Owned and preserved by the AMA Motorcycle Heritage Museum, this 1967 T100R is the factory racer that Dick Hammer rode to near victory in the 1967 Daytona 200. In 1968 it was acquired by Texas Triumph dealer Woody Leone Sr., and ridden by Skip Van Leeuwen, AMA national number 59.

necting rods were added, along with a full-flow oil filter to protect the bearing surfaces.

Something on the order of 200 Grand Prix models were produced between 1948 and 1950, when the racing model was replaced with a racing kit so anyone could produce his own Triumph Grand Prix. In a pattern that would be followed for as long as there were Triumphs, many of the special high-performance bikes and racing kits made their way across the pond to power-hungry Yanks.

## Birth of the Trophy

It is interesting to note that Edward Turner considered trials events of the day a good test of reliability, and thus different from road racing. As such he was more willing to allow and even encourage factory participation in events of this type.

In 1948, Triumph riders won the International Six Days Trial on modified Tiger 100s. These used the same winning combination first tried by Freddie Clarke, a generator top-end mated to a Tiger 100 bottom end. As happened with the Grand Prix, success of the race biker created a new model, the TR5 "Trophy." While the hastily assembled factory bikes relied on nearly stock rigid frames with sprung hubs in the rear, the new TR5 models came with special reinforced frames with a shorter wheelbase.

The new Triumph Trophys came with lights, though these were designed to be easily removed for competition use. And though the engine came in a mild state of tune for low-speed work, the availability of the racing kit meant you could extract considerably more power from the 500-cc twin-cylinder engine. With a wide-ratio four-speed gearbox, the Trophy was ideal for off-road events, though it still made a nice light street-scrambler machine as well.

With the fairing lower removed, you can see the special magnesium timing gear cover, the Chevrolet Corvair oil cooler, and the Lucas 3ET racing ignition unit.

When the close-pitch top ends were added to the T100 line, the Trophys got the same new components and in 1955 the TR5 received a frame with true swinging arm rear suspension. By 1956 there were two Trophys, the TR5 and the new TR6, powered by the larger 650-cc engine. Both remained immensely popular through the next decade. One of the last uses of the Trophy name was on the new 500-cc dirt model known as the Trophy Trail, produced in limited numbers for the 1973 and 1974 model years.

### Stateside Racing

Starting with the first Grand Prix models, any high-performance Triumphs were produced with an eye to the American market. American racing included both off-road events like Trials and Desert racing, as well as road racing at tracks like Daytona.

For off-road events, first the TR5 Trophy and then the TR6 were often the machines of choice, due to their powerful engines, light weight and durable drive trains.

In the early 1950s, Tiger 100-mounted riders won their share of U.S. road races. In 1953, Triumph offered the T100 in a C (or competition) designation, and factory-backed rider Ed Fisher won the AMA National road race at Laconia, New Hampshire.

And though Edward Turner was officially opposed to racing, the factory did build some

Triumph's hybrid 500-cc models—as shown in the 1948 TR5—are very rare today. Note the square shape of the cylinder head and barrel—carryovers from wartime RAF generator use. The undrilled mounting bosses on the barrel's side were originally used to mount the generator's cooling shroud. This 1948 engine is upgraded for vintage trials with a nonstandard Amal Concentric carburetor and modern high-tension ignition leads. In 1951 the TR5 was fitted with the new round profile, "close pitch" die-cast cylinder and head.

This 1956 TR5R is one of only 112 hand-built at the factory to run in U.S. road races like Daytona. Though the factory used a stock Tiger 100 frame, the front forks were borrowed from the Trophy line.

The rare TR5R racer is an original bike, as proven by the serial number stamping. Note the twin Amal carbs and magneto ignition. The intake tracts, originally parallel as made by the factory, were converted into a splayed arrangement by American Triumph tuner Cliff Guild.

"works specials" during the mid-1950s. In 1955, Triumph built a short run of T100/R bikes intended for Class C competition against Harleys and BSAs. The close-pitch 500-cc twins came equipped with dual carburetors, magneto ignition and the small, 2.5-gallon fuel tank, all set in a TR5 rigid frame.

For road racers Triumph offered a similar bike, the TR5R. In 1956, the factory built only 112 of these bikes, and the majority were shipped to Triumph's most important market, America. Instead of the rigid frame used on the T100/R, the road-race bikes used the new swingarm frame introduced in 1954, combined with a special, certified dual-carb 500-cc engine. Built by hand in the extreme, each engine came with E3134 high lift cams, bronze valve guides, 9:1 compression pistons and a Lucas racing magneto.

Though the T100R came with no brakes, the TR5R featured the eight-inch front brake from the larger TR6 as well as its small, detachable headlight. At about this time Triumph was developing the new "Delta" head for the 500-cc twins. This alloy head was set up for two carbs in a splayed-port configuration instead of the parallel ports of the standard twin-carb cylinder head. The new head also featured larger, 1.5-inch intake valves to further enhance the engine's breathing ability.

In 1957, the TR5R was replaced by the T100RS, a production road racer that came with the new Delta head and a five-gallon gas tank borrowed from the Thunderbird line.

## Do It in the Dirt

With or without the help of factory specials, Triumph owners always did well with TT racing,

The replica's 500-cc engine uses a billet crankshaft and stock rods with Hepolite pistons. Pistons and combustion chambers are modified to provide a "squish band" similar to the factory set-up developed by Triumph engineer Doug Hele. Carbs are Amal MkII; pipes and megaphones are built by hand.

Inspired by the number 59 bike now in the AMA Museum, John and Tom Healy from Coventry Spares in Massachusetts set out a few years ago to build a replica. Poised at Daytona prior to a recent AHRMA race, their number 3 bike uses mostly stock components in place of the one-off exotica developed by the factory in 1967. The bike is based on a stock T100R frame, modified to accept the alloy oil tank, racing gas tank, and Ceriani forks.

even against supposedly faster brands with larger engines. The first TT winners for Triumph were T100 bikes with the generator or Grand Prix top end. Some early TT winners did the job on nearly stock Thunderbirds. Later, the winning ticket for TT fame became a modified TR6, and eventually one of the "specials" purpose-built at the factory to suit American needs.

This very rare T120C TT dates from 1963—the first year these special bikes were available. This Western-style, off-road Triumph came with a special competition engine, no headlight, and a tachometer. With 12:1 compression and wild cams, this 650 put out more power than a stock Bonneville. Carbs are 376 Amals (same as a Bonneville) though this C bike uses Energy Transfer ignition. High-level straight pipes like these were only used on the TT Bonnies during 1963 and 1964. The "Made in England" decal on the frame tube, though popular with restorers, was not fitted by Triumph until the 1971 model year.

Triumph's success in off-road events prompted the factory to produce a series of specials based on both the Bonneville and TR6 bikes. Starting in 1963 the company offered a special T120C model, aimed at American-style TT Steeplechase, Hare Scrambles and desert events. It was armed with 12:1 compression, a pair of Amal Monobloc carburetors and standard Bonneville gearing. Exhaust for the first years passed through straight pipes mounted high, with one on each side of the bike.

In 1965, the long straight pipes were swapped for short pipes that ran down and along the lower frame tube on either side of the bike. In 1966 the C designation was dropped and the bikes became known by the name most racers called them, TT Special. The model dominated TT racing on every level for many years after production ended in 1967. As author Lindsay Brooke put it, "The broad torque and balanced chassis of Meriden's large twin made it the consummate TT tool."

The company also offered a single-carb, TR6-based off-road equivalent to the T120 C and TT models, known as the TR6SC. Designed for reliability rather than top speed, the TR6SC was powered by a stock engine and straight pipes mounted high on either side or with both running together down the left side in 1966. Known to U.S. motorcyclists as a "desert sled," the TR6 was the winningest machine ever turned loose on the wide-open Western landscape.

One of the "top guns" for Triumph in the 1960s and early 1970s, Gene Romero is seen on his flat track bike in 1971. The bike is a 750-kitted Triumph twin with special dirt-track primary cover, mounted in a Trackmaster chassis. *Lindsay Brooke collection*

This triple of modern construction is very close to the factory bikes raced during the early 1970s. The bike started as a chassis kit complete with fairing, from Miles Engineering in England. Number 414 uses a Rob North-style "low boy" frame and 1971-style fairing, both near duplicates of factory equipment used when the triples won at Daytona. Three-cylinder engine uses 30mm Amal carburetors, electronic ignition, and Megacycle cams with the same specs as those used by Doug Hele on the factory racers.

mier American race the Triumph factory produced a series of special triples. Each used a frame built by specialist Rob North, surrounded by an equally new wind-tunnel-designed fairing.

Triumph's new racers came to the track with 80-horsepower engines. Eleven-to-one compres-

sion, three Amal 1 and 3/16-inch GP carbs, over-size intakes, some careful porting work, and light-weight valve hardware are some of the details that separated these bikes from stock Tridents. If that wasn't enough, the lower ends came with improved oiling and polished rods. One of the bike's big

The Murray/Manning streamliner at Bonneville, 1973. Equipped with two Boris Murray-built pre-unit engines with Chantland big bore kits and twin-carb heads, it was fueled with 80 percent nitromethane. The bike went well over 270 miles per hour before crashing. *Lindsay Brooke collection*

power secrets was the exhaust system, which used the first three-into-one collector-style headers on a factory race bike.

Despite the fact that the Triumph effort was a limited, first-year effort, the new triples placed second and third at Daytona that first year. One year later the BSA/Triumph team came back—with one of the biggest, most sophisticated racing teams ever assembled at Daytona.

The 1971 bikes included a group from the past year and four new mounts. The newest of the bikes came with new "low boy" Rob North frames, new cylinder heads, higher compression, and specially modified 30-mm Amal Concentric carburetors. In the end the three-cylinder BSA/Triumph team took the top three places. But BSA Group's financial troubles meant that there would never be another year like 1971. Only one year later the BSA/Triumph win seemed like ancient history

when the best finish for either a BSA or Triumph was sixth place.

## Triumph Earns the Bonneville Name

The inspiration for the name Bonneville, and the script, "World's Fastest Motorcycle" came on those legendary Utah Salt Flats starting in 1955. Though there were record-breaking Triumphs before that, 1955 was the year dirt-track rider Johnny Allen piloted a Triumph engine streamliner built by Jack Wilson and Stormy Mangham to a record 193.30 miles per hour. Known first as the *Devil's Arrow*, then the *Texas Cee-gar*, the relatively simple machine used a modified Thunderbird 650 engine set into a long streamliner built around a light airplane frame.

Early in the summer of 1956, a large team from the German NSU factory came to the Salt Flats with a very sophisticated streamliner powered

Big D Cycle of Dallas, Texas, has brought a variety of Triumphs to the Utah salt over the last 40 years, including this single engine Trident-powered bike with Jon Minonno as rider. *Lindsay Brooke collection*

by a blown NSU vertical twin. The massive factory effort broke Johnny Allen's record with a new two-way average of 210.77 miles per hour.

Not to be outdone by a bunch of Europeans, Jack Wilson and crew returned to the salt later that summer of 1956 with a much improved *Cee-gar.* Still relying on the old T-bird twin, the stock crank was swapped for a one-piece billet crank and Triumph rods were used, but with Cadillac bearings in the big end. Two Amal GP carbs fed air and fuel to an improved and modified T-bird head.

The head itself used modified Harley-Davidson valves and S&W springs. For camshafts the boys from Texas chose high-lift Triumph "Q" cams. Running on a mixture of 60 percent nitro, the improved American streamliner set a new record at 214.17 miles per hour. For a variety of reasons—none of them understandable to Americans—the Federation International Motorcycliste (FIM)

refused to accept the speed run as the official world's record.

With or without the blessing of the FIM, Triumph legitimately claimed the title of World's Fastest Motorcycle. To prove the point, Edward Turner named his new 1959 model the Bonneville, and each bike carried the decal, "World's Fastest Motorcycle."

Triumph-powered motorcycles consistently ratcheted the top-speed record higher and higher. *Gyronaut,* one of the best-known of the streamliners, used two Triumph engines to extend the record, first to 217 miles per hour, then all the way to 245 miles per hour in 1966.

After that a variety of Triumph-powered machines chased, and sometimes broke, the ever-increasing top speed record. One twin-engine machine, the Manning/Murray streamliner, went through the timing lights at 277 miles per hour in

The Metisse was created by the Rickman brothers for off-road competition. Fork is from Ceriani, wheels measure 21 inches in front and 18 in the rear. This example from 1968 was completely restored with even the frame renickeled.

1973, while sliding on its side on the salt. Because of the crash, and engine troubles the next day, the machine never made the required two-way run to establish a new record.

In addition to holding the "World's Fastest" title for 15 years, Triumph-powered motorcycles have set, and still hold, records in a variety of classes. Perennial "salty dogs" like Jack Wilson and Big D Cycle in Texas have set and broken records in every imaginable class, running everything from single-engine 500-cc twins to twin-engine, turbocharged triples.

Dirt, asphalt, or salt, Triumph-powered motorcycles won and established records in nearly every type of racing. All this in spite of the early opposition from none other than the man who ran the company. The many successes serve as further testimony to the strength of the original design, and the enthusiasm of the men and women who rode and sold Triumph motorcycles.

This Metisse is equipped with a 500-cc unit engine (many were built with 650-cc power), in a mild state of tune, with a single carburetor and unusual exhaust system.

Triumph's production-racing Thruxton Bonneville is a rare piece indeed. Special bits abounded on the roughly 70 examples the factory built. Thruxtons were built in fits and starts from 1965 to 1969. Classic Bike/*EMAP Archives*

Triumph engines have long formed the basis for various specials, with the Triton (Triumph engine, Norton featherbed frame) always one of the most popular. The Dresda Triton shown was built by Dave Degens, well-known English racer and owner of the Dresda Autos shop. *Nick Nicholls*

A rare, 1972 Rickman-framed triple—one of only 10 known to have been built. The bike competes in AHRMA Vintage Sportsman 750 and Vintage Formula classes.

The engine in the Rickman three-cylinder racer uses a Big D Cycle cylinder head, fed by three 30-mm Amal carburetors, and Carrillo connecting rods to ensure longevity.

# CHAPTER 6

# THE NEW TRIUMPHS

## The Phoenix Rises

When it seemed Triumph was finally finished, that it had reinvented itself for the final time and shipped the last Bonneville, there was in fact one more ray of hope.

That ray carried the name John Bloor. An English industrialist, Bloor bought the Triumph name soon after Meriden's closure in 1983, though he had no real intention of producing the vertical twins everyone associated with Triumph. Instead, he briefly licensed the production of Bonnevilles to Les Harris, who ran a small Triumph aftermarket parts company. In this way the Bonneville was given a five-year extension on its death sentence.

The larger plan, however, called for Triumph to become the maker of thoroughly modern motorcycles. Bikes with three- and four-cylinder engines, current styling and bulletproof reliability.

Anyone looking for a bit of Edward Turner in the new designs was disappointed. The new Triumph company started with a clean sheet of paper, a brand-new factory in Hinckley, Leicestershire, England, and a series of new designs. The only

Triumph's answer to the cafe racer is the Speed Triple, seen here in its pre-1997 form. Prior to the introduction of the T509, the Speed Triple utilized the steel frame, sheet metal, and three cylinder carbureted engine common to much of the Triumph line.

thing left from the old days are some of the model names and the retro styling of two models.

Everything else is squeaky clean and new. In order to reduce inventories and tooling costs, the new company started with a modular plan that makes the most of two basic engine layouts.

What these bikes have in common is a three- or four-cylinder engine with dual overhead camshafts, one carburetor per cylinder, a five- or six-speed transmission and liquid cooling. By sharing parts, Triumph could produce three-cylinder bikes of 750 and 900 cc, and four-cylinder machines of 1,000 and 1,200 cc. All these use a steel frame with conventional Showa forks in front and a single shock in back supporting an aluminum swingarm with eccentric axle adjusters.

With careful juggling of components and great marketing, the new corporation created a whole line of motorcycles. The new line of Triumphs included everything from simple unfaired triples to fully faired superbikes, all with a large percentage of shared components.

Critics have charged that while the new Triumph Motorcycles Ltd. has indeed introduced world-class bikes under the old name, the rate of model change has slowed greatly since the initial introductions. In answer to such charges, Triumph introduced a series of significantly improved three-cylinder bikes for the 1997 model year.

Offered without a fairing, the three-cylinder Trident is one of the least-expensive Triumphs. Yet the buyer still gets dual disc brakes, a six-speed transmission, single-shock rear suspension, and an overhead cam engine with 90 or 97 horsepower.

The T595 Daytona and T509 Speed Triple are part of what Triumph calls its "attack on the supersports market." The all-new three-cylinder engine used for the T595 displaces 955 cc, from a 79 x 65-mm bore and stroke. For the T509 a very similar engine displaces the familiar 885 cc (often called a 900-cc engine). Both use a redesigned cylinder head, increased compression and a sophisticated engine-management system to boost both power and rideability. These are thoroughly modern engines and proof that the new Triumph is alive and well. Ironically, these more exotic models are made possible by the success of the much more conservative bikes first produced by the reborn company.

## The Trident

The Trident is, in essence, Triumph's entry-level bike. Equipped with the basic water-cooled three-cylinder engine in either 750- or 900-cc displacements, this unfaired machine is one of Triumph's most popular models. The two displacements are obtained from essentially the same engine by changing only the stroke. While Triumph's current 750-cc engines use bore and stroke dimensions of 76 x 55 mm, the 900-cc engines retain the 76-mm bore and increase the stroke to 65 mm.

Each cylinder, no matter what its displacement, is fed through a single Mikuni flat-slide, constant-velocity carburetor. The aluminum cylinder head uses four valves per cylinder, operated by twin overhead camshafts, chain driven off the engine's right side.

Though this might be the Chevy Bel Air of the line, the small Trident is rated at 90 horsepower at 10,000 rpm (the 900 is rated at 97 horsepower). This least-powerful Triumph still attains 68 foot-pounds of torque at 8,700 rpm and uses a redline of

Triumph's entry into the large-displacement sportbike wars is the Daytona 1200. Equipped with the modular plan's 1,200-cc four-cylinder variant, the bike is equipped with its own fairing, the steel frame used on other models, the deluxe version of the 41mm forks, and single-shock rear suspension.

11,000 rpm. All Tridents come with dual front disc brakes, a single disc in back, a six-speed transmission, and chain drive. Conventional 43-mm forks support the front end while a single, adjustable shock with rising-rate linkage is used in back. Six-spoke alloy wheels are used on both ends.

Though it might be the least-expensive Triumph, the Trident isn't lacking for much, which helps to explain the early success of this three-cylinder machine.

### Daytona

Named after the famous American race track (and the older 500-cc twin that was, in fact, named after the track) this is the top-of-the-line Triumph.

Up until 1997, the Daytonas came to consumers with the familiar 900- and 1,200-cc, three- and four-cylinder configurations. The standard three-cylinder Daytona engine used the same 76 x 65-mm bore and stroke dimensions, equipped with the same three CV carburetors, and the same 10.6:1 compression seen in the other Triumph triples.

A higher output motor, rated at 113 horsepower, set the Super III Daytona apart from its more mundane little brother. In addition to having more power, the Super III came with more brakes, in the form of two six-piston calipers in front squeezing 310 mm floating rotors.

The 1200-cc Daytona was created by adding one cylinder to the 900-cc engine. This is not as easy as it sounds, and Triumph did keep everything as simple as possible by using many pieces from the three-cylinder engine. Thus the bore and stroke dimensions, the carburetors, and the valves are all identical between the two engines. You could say the 1,200-cc engine has all the same stuff—just

more of it—and a higher compression ratio to provide a final output of 145 horsepower.

All the pre-1997 Daytonas use the same steel frame with aluminum swingarm equipped with eccentric axle adjusters. While the less-expensive bikes use a single rear shock adjustable for preload only, the premier models like the Daytona allow the user to adjust rebound damping as well. In front, the Daytona bikes use the 43-mm fork assembly seen on other models, but adjustable for compression and rebound damping, as well as preload. Both the 900- and 1,200-cc bikes use dual 310-mm discs squeezed by four-piston calipers.

## Enter the T595

For 1997 Triumph introduced a new Daytona model, the T595. Not just a re-painted Super III, the T595 is a new motorcycle guaranteed to silence the critics and get everyone's full attention.

Start with the frame. Instead of the steel frame used in various forms on many of Triumph's bikes, the new model uses a perimeter frame made of oval-shaped aluminum tubing. The new chassis is lighter, shorter by almost two inches, and equipped with a single-sided swingarm in the rear.

Set into that frame is the real news of the T595, the new three-cylinder engine. Triumph needed more power and less weight. The new crankcases are lighter by 22 pounds, the company claims, and use magnesium or plastic for many of the covers. Though the stroke remains the same at 65 mm, the bore is new at 79 mm for a total displacement of 955 cc. The new cylinder head comes with larger, lighter valves and more compression. In lieu of Mikuni CV carburetors, the new triple is equipped with fuel injection controlled by a computerized engine-management system that handles the ignition as well as the fuel.

The T595 utilizes a sexy single-sided swingarm, single-shock rear suspension and three-spoke, 17-inch wheel shod with a Bridgestone 190/50 tire. Fully adjustable front forks measure 45 mm and support the 120/70 x 17 Bridgestone tire. Front brakes use dual, four-piston calipers matched to 320 mm floating rotors.

The new-for-1997 Daytona T595 is a whole new motorcycle. Gone is the previous Daytona's steel frame, carbureted engine and fairing with two round headlights. The T595 comes with an aluminum frame, fuel injected 955-cc three-cylinder engine, and a more aerodynamic fairing.

Equipped with a new fairing and a screaming-yellow paint job, the T595 offers more power in a lighter package. It's a cutting-edge bike that shows another dimension to the new Triumph.

## Thunderbird

The Thunderbird uses traditional-looking sheet metal and an even more traditional name to create the modern Triumph cruiser. While the rest of the line (with the exception of the closely related Adventurer) borrows very little from the earlier bikes, the Thunderbird uses a gas tank with the signature shape, a 1960s style twinseat, spoked wheels, and plenty of chrome. The overall appearance is aimed at riders who want the traditional beauty of a Thunderbird or Bonneville twin from

A blend of old and new—and a motorcycle that's very different from most of the modern bikes currently offered by Triumph. The Thunderbird uses a mildly tuned version of the 900-cc engine with five-speed gearbox to complement the timeless and very American styling theme. Note the spoked wheels, old-style tank badge, "dual exhaust," large-diameter headlight, stand-alone gauges in their chrome housings and the twinseat. All the right stuff for a modern cruiser named Thunderbird.

the old days, without the mechanical hassles of maintaining a 40-some year-old bike.

Beneath the retro styling, however, beats a modern three-cylinder heart. In the best modular manner, the new T-bird uses the same 900-cc engine seen in the Trident and Sprint, with just slightly less horsepower at high rpm and slightly more torque at lower engine speeds.

The steel-spine frame used for the T-bird is also shared with the Adventurer. In front is the same 43-mm fork used on many of the modern Triumph mounts, and in back the same single-shock rear suspension. For the T-bird only one disc brake is used up front with one more in back. And though the more sporting bikes give the rider six gears to choose from, the Thunderbird cruiser rider is only allowed a range of five cogs. Like the rest of the line, gears are used for primary drive, with a chain final drive.

## Speed Triple

Prior to the 1997 models, the Speed Triple shared the steel frame and 900-cc engine with other members of the Triumph team. Offered as a bare bike and dressed as a cafe racer, the Speed Triple used the 43-mm fork and the single-shock rear suspension both with adjustable preload and damping. In keeping with the sporting nature of the bike, the larger, 310-mm floating front rotors are used with four-piston calipers on either front fork leg.

When Triumph created the new Daytona T595, much of the same hardware and technology was used to create the 1997 Speed Triple T509. The new Speed Triple uses the "old" bore and stroke dimension of 76 x 65 mm, but otherwise uses all the new bits and pieces offered on the T595. Fed by fuel injection and equipped with the new cylinder head, the 900-cc engine is rated at 108 horsepower.

The same aluminum perimeter frame used on the T595 is used here, with the same single-sided swingarm and fully adjustable 45-mm front fork. In keeping with the cafe racer theme, the Speed Triple comes as a bare-bike painted either Lucifer Orange or Jet Black.

The new Triumphs are just that—new. They borrow very little from the Edward Turner era, though that isn't all bad. The first three- and four-cylinder designs have proved both popular and reliable. Today, Triumphs are sold in nearly every corner of the globe. In early 1996, the 40,000th new Triumph was shipped to a dealer in Australia.

Critics who charged the new company with moving too slowly have been silenced by the

With almost no components borrowed from the modular Triumph line, the new-for-1997 T509 Speed Triple utilizes the aluminum frame and suspension from the T595, equipped with a fuel-injected 900-cc three-cylinder engine.

The 900-cc Tiger was introduced in 1993, bringing the "desert sled" concept into the 90s.

introduction of the awesome T595 and T509. If he was still alive, Edward Turner would have a smile on his face today at the success of the new Triumph Motorcycles Ltd. Turner always made the most of a good design, shared parts among models wherever possible, and then used that momentum to fuel the introduction of new, cutting-edge machines.

# INDEX